FACT FILE: JELLYFISH

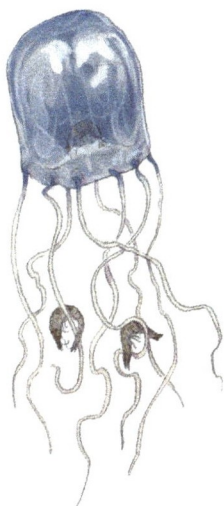

By JBus

Library For All Ltd.

LIBRARY FOR ALL
DIGITAL EDUCATION FOR THE WORLD

Library For All is an Australian not for profit organisation with a mission to make knowledge accessible to all via an innovative digital library solution. Visit us at libraryforall.org

Fact File: Jellyfish

First published 2023

Published by Library For All Ltd
Email: info@libraryforall.org
URL: libraryforall.org

Our Yarning logo design by Jason Lee, Bidjipidji Art

Original illustrations by Kit Turner

Fact File: Jellyfish
JBus
ISBN: 978-1-923143-12-8
SKU04314

FACT FILE:
JELLYFISH

We respect and honour Aboriginal
and Torres Strait Islander Elders past,
present and future. We acknowledge
the stories, traditions and living cultures
of Aboriginal and Torres Strait Islander
peoples on this land and commit to
building a brighter future together.

Contents

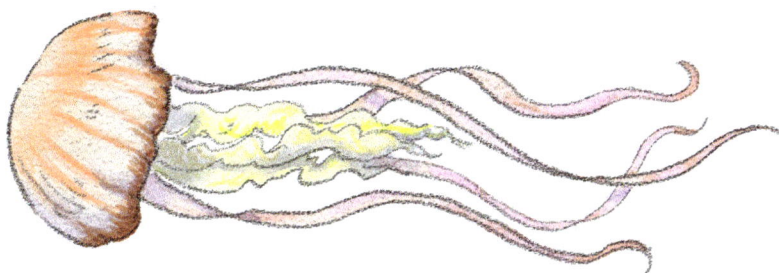

Appearance

Jellyfish come in all the colours of the rainbow. Some are transparent, while others are pink, blue, orange, or even green! They can be bioluminescent as well, meaning they can produce their own light.

Jellyfish have large blobby heads known as hoods or bells. They also have tentacles that can sting or even kill other animals. Jellyfish grab onto prey or predators using their thicker tentacles known as oral arms. Their mouths are in the middle of their body, underneath the hood, and are protected by both tentacles and oral arms.

The strangest thing about jellyfish is they don't have a heart or a brain!

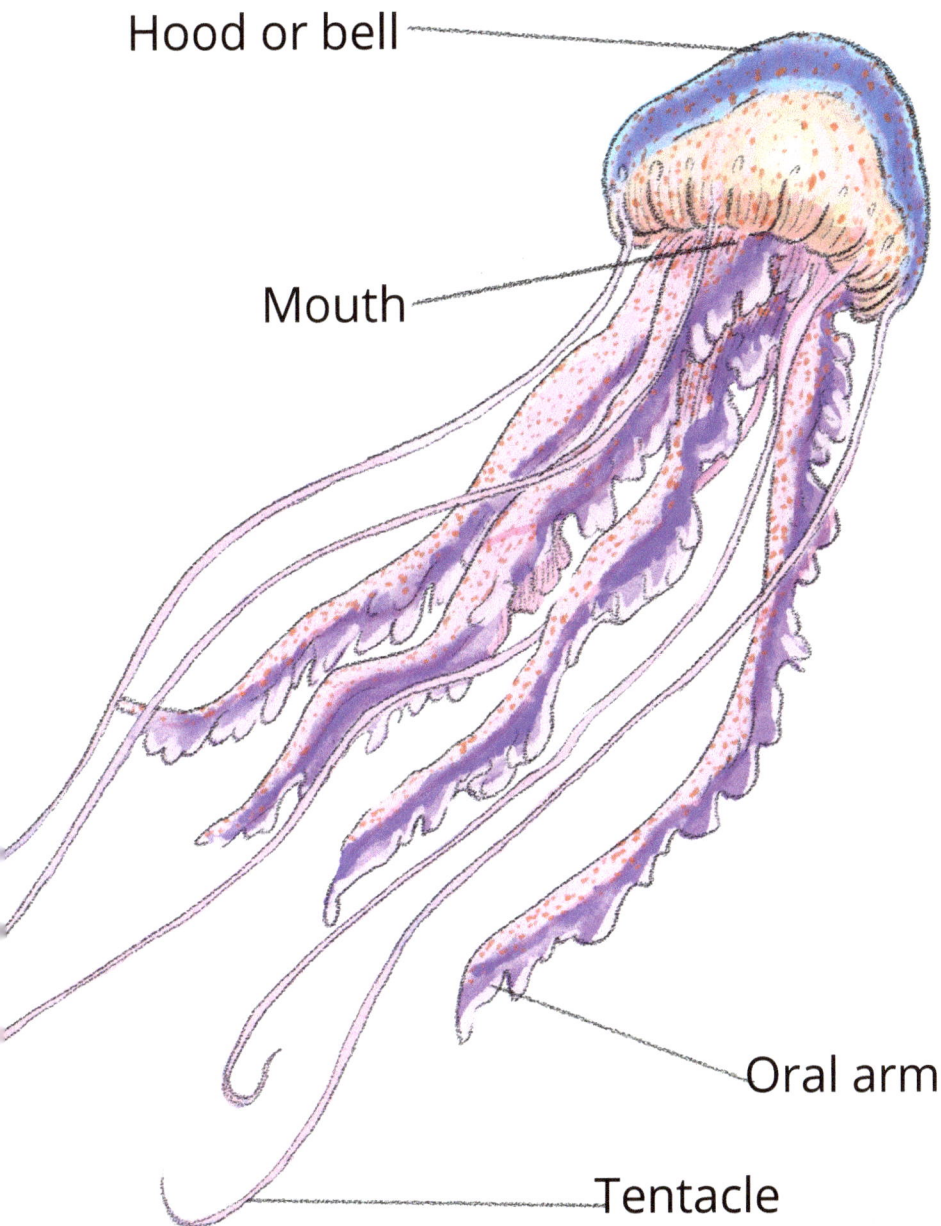

Hood or bell

Mouth

Oral arm

Tentacle

Jellyfish are invertebrates because they don't have a backbone, or any bones at all. They are made of 95 per cent water, which is why they can float in ocean currents so easily.

Their life span is not long. Most jellyfish only live for one to two years, though some live much longer.

Jellyfish can weigh up to two kilograms.

Most are around one centimetre wide; except, the Lion's Mane Jellyfish is three feet wide!

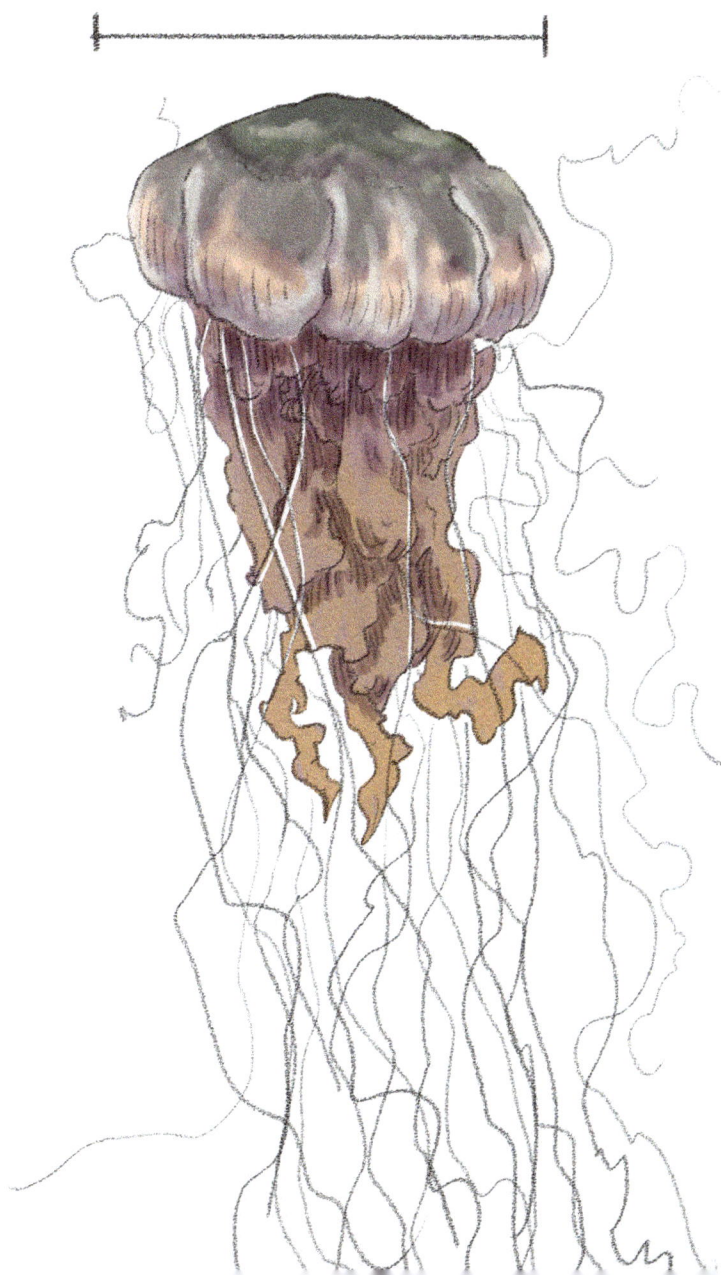

Eating Habits

Jellyfish are carnivores, which means they only eat meat. They'll eat any organism that can fit in their mouth, including shrimp, plankton, crabs, small fish, and other jellyfish.

Young jellyfish can eat plants to help them grow, such as seaweed and algae. However, meat is the standard food for jellyfish. No matter their age, all jellyfish eat through the only cavity in their body: a hidden mouth that is the same hole they poo through.

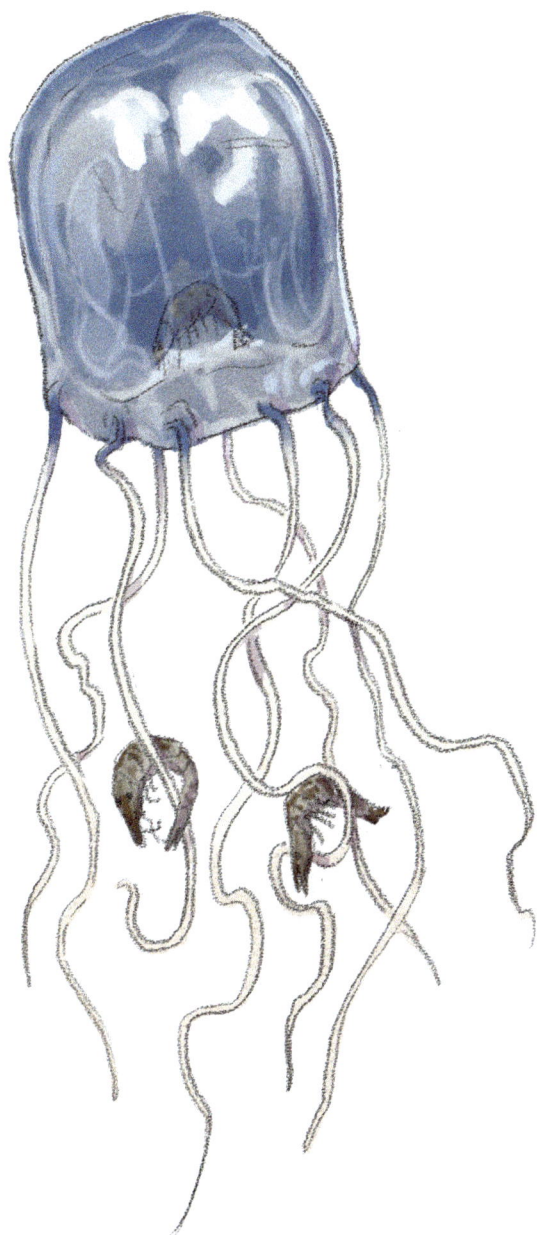

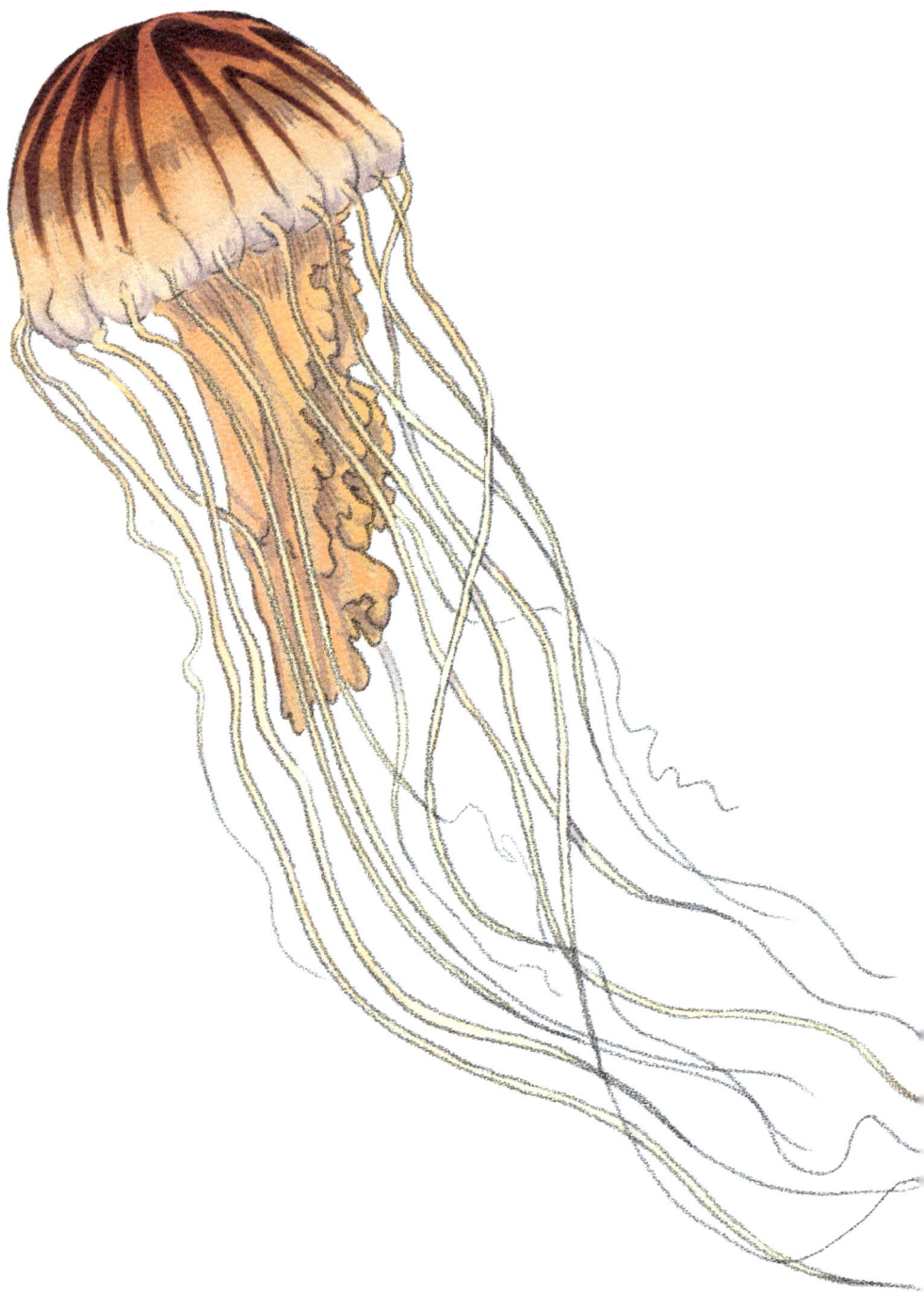

Habitat

Jellyfish live all over the world in the oceans and in fresh waterways. Depending on their species, they can acclimate to live in cold and warm waters. This allows them to live along coastlines and deep in the sea.

Predators

It's surprising how many predators would like to have jellyfish for dinner. They don't look very tasty, after all! The list includes:

- turtles, especially the leatherback sea turtle
- seabirds, such as fulmars
- whale sharks
- ocean sunfish
- grey triggerfish.

To avoid being eaten, the jellyfish can camouflage itself in the clear water by turning its body transparent. As a last resort, they can also use the stingers in their tentacles to hurt predators.

Reproduction

Jellyfish reproduction is a little different to other animals. Some jellyfish create and fertilise their eggs inside their bodies, while others release eggs into the water to be fertilised by other jellyfish. If they're healthy, jellyfish can release eggs once a day.

Baby jellyfish

Fertilised eggs can become jellyfish in two ways. They either hatch into tiny worms called planulae and swim around, or they can settle on a rock and enter a polyp stage of growth. This polyp stage can create more than one baby jellyfish at a time, whereas the worm stage does not.

These baby jellyfish feed on plankton, algae, and seaweed until they are big enough to eat meat.

More fun facts
- There are 2000 species of jellyfish and 70 of them are dangerous to humans.
- The most dangerous jellyfish species are the Box Jellyfish and the Irukandji Jellyfish.
- Jellyfish can swim at a speed of eight kilometres an hour.
- Groups of jellyfish are called a bloom, a swarm, or a smack of jellyfish.
- Jellyfish do not have a fixed gender. They change between male and female throughout their lives.
- Jellyfish are technically not fish.
- There is a type of jellyfish called the Immortal Jellyfish. When it dies, it falls to the bottom of the ocean and decays. Then, it comes back to life, regenerating as a polyp.

Glossary

Word	Meaning
Bioluminescent	An organism that produces its own light with no heat
Invertebrates	Organisms with no spinal column/backbone
Carnivore	A creature that only eats meat
Species	A group of organisms with biological and physical similarities
Fertilise	Cause a new organism to develop by applying male reproductive material to female reproductive material
Camouflage	To blend in with the environment
Polyp	The stage of growth where the egg has settled on a rock and can create multiple jellyfish

You can use these questions to talk about this book with your family, friends and teachers.

What did you learn from this book?

Describe this book in one word.
Funny? Scary? Colourful? Interesting?

How did this book make you feel when you finished reading it?

What was your favourite part of this book?

download our reader app
getlibraryforall.org

About the author

JBus is a Kabi Kabi woman from Queensland and lives in Brisbane. She enjoys being at the beach with her family, creating art and singing.

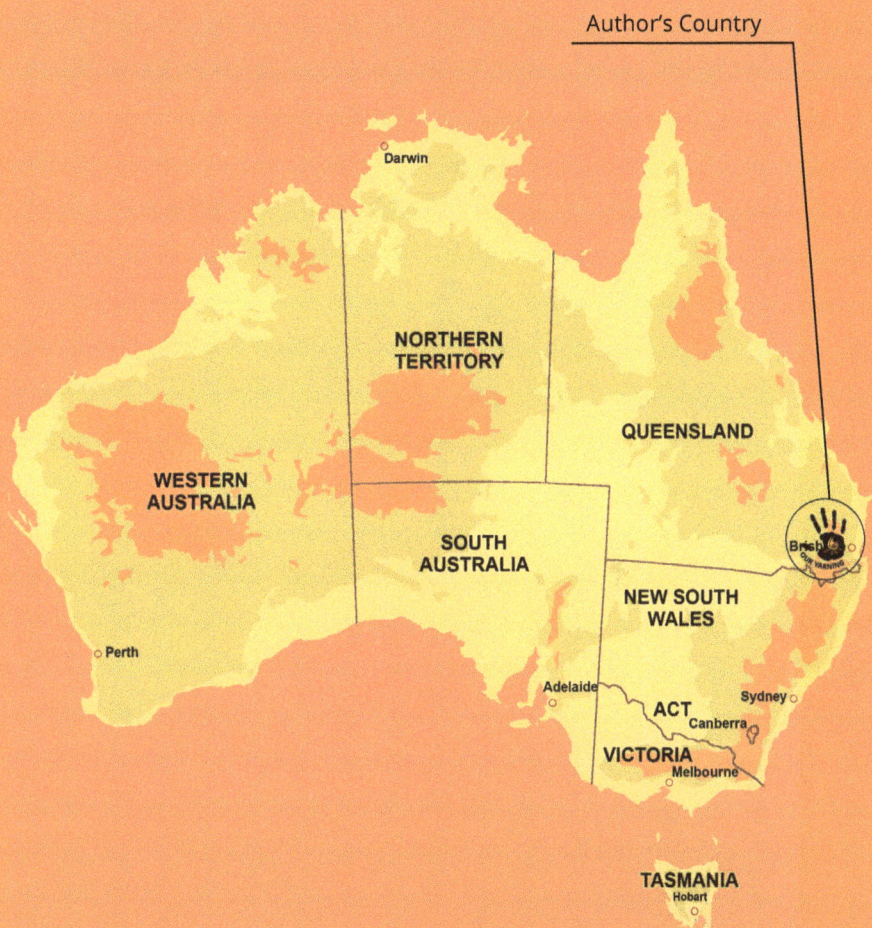

Author's Country

Darwin

NORTHERN TERRITORY

QUEENSLAND

WESTERN AUSTRALIA

SOUTH AUSTRALIA

NEW SOUTH WALES

Perth

Adelaide

Sydney

ACT
Canberra

VICTORIA
Melbourne

Brisbane

TASMANIA
Hobart

Our Yarning

Want to discover more books from this collection? Our Yarning is a collection of books written by Aboriginal and Torres Strait Islander peoples across Australia.

We know that children learn better, and enjoy reading more, when they see themselves in the stories, characters and illustrations of the books they read.

To download the app, visit the Google Play Store on any Android device and search 'Our Yarning'.